DO YOU KNOW?

SHARKS

Scholastic Children's Books,
Euston House, 24 Eversholt Street,
London NW1 1DB, UK

A division of Scholastic Ltd
London ~ New York ~ Toronto ~ Sydney ~ Auckland
Mexico City ~ New Delhi ~ Hong Kong

Published in the UK by Scholastic Ltd, 2013

Text © Helen Greathead, 2013
Illustrations © Tom Connell, 2013

ISBN 978 1407 12185 7

Printed and bound in the UK by CPI Group (UK) Ltd, Croydon, CR0 4YY

2 4 6 8 10 9 7 5 3 1

DO YOU KNOW...

- how to hypnotize a shark?

- whether sharks have friends?

- why some sharks eat people?

No? Then keep reading and you'll soon find out...

Incredible sharks!

Sharks are the biggest fish in the sea, but not all are huge and dangerous. There are 300 to 400 different types of shark. They divide up into lots of smaller families that look and behave differently. But all sharks have some features that are the same...

• a skeleton made from cartilage, not bone. It is lightweight and bendy, like the hard parts of our noses and ears

• **skin covered with small, hard scales, called denticles**

• five to seven gill slits on each side of its body. A shark has to swim forward to push water into its mouth. It gets oxygen from the water and pushes carbon dioxide out through its gill slits

• A very large liver that is filled with oil. The oil is lighter than water, so it keeps the shark afloat...

A shark's whole body is designed to move through water smoothly and easily:

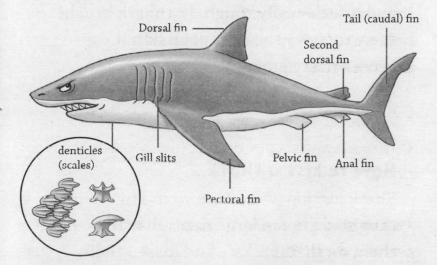

Dorsal fin

Second dorsal fin

Tail (caudal) fin

denticles (scales)

Gill slits

Pelvic fin

Anal fin

Pectoral fin

The denticles on a shark's skin are coated with enamel — the same stuff that coats our teeth!

DO YOU KNOW?

Shark friends?

How to stroke a shark...

Stroke a shark towards its tail and it feels smooth and silky. Stroke towards its nose and it feels really rough. If a shark brushes the wrong way against your skin it can leave a nasty graze.

How to kiss a shark...

Shark kissing was a custom in Fiji! Men caught sharks in large nets. They turned them on their backs – and kissed their tummies! They believed that kissing a shark would calm it down, so it would never attack a human. Did they hypnotize the shark? See page 69.

How NOT to kiss a shark...

One dive group leader claimed he often stroked sharks and sometimes even kissed them. But in 2006, when he tried kissing a nurse shark, it turned round and bit him very hard on the lips – ouch!

THE TOP 3

Unexpected places to find sharks

Sharks live in all kinds of different conditions. You'll find them in seas just about anywhere in the world.

3. Lemon sharks don't like the deep. Instead they lurk in the shallow reefs, bays and mangrove swamps of warm, tropical waters, waiting to catch shellfish, and other sharks for their tea.

2. The Portuguese shark doesn't just live near Portugal, it's found in seas as far away as Japan and New Zealand. It lives deeper in the ocean than any other shark — at up to 3,600 metres below!

1. The Greenland shark is the only shark that can survive in the Arctic Circle. It swims in dark, ice-covered waters for most of the year. It's a big shark, but it moves very slowly most of the time, which is why some people call it a sleeper shark.

But you wouldn't ever find a shark in a river would you...?

... well, mind your toes, because bull sharks really can live in fresh water and sea water. They have been found...

- **in the Ganges River, in India**
- **in the Mississippi River, in North America**
- **in the Amazon River, in South America, a whopping 2,500 miles from the sea!**

Experts think the sharks find fresh water a safer place for their babies to grow up – away from other sharks that might want to eat them!

Cruising the ocean

Just like birds, and many other animals, some types of shark migrate. They swim long distances to find – or follow – their food source, to have babies or to stay away from danger.

Blue sharks swim in nearly all seas. They are really good at migration. Each year Caribbean blue sharks take a fantastic trip from the  Caribbean, along the US coast, across to Europe, down to the north coast of Africa then back to the Caribbean again.

One great white shark was nicknamed Nicole, after actress and shark fan, Nicole Kidman. Nicole, the shark, was tagged and recorded swimming from South Africa to Australia. She swam 6,800 miles in 99 days travelling at just under 3 miles per hour.

South Africa
3,400 miles

Australia
3,400 miles

Migration mysteries

For years, UK scientists wondered where basking sharks disappeared to in the winter. One expert suggested that they hibernated on the ocean floor.

In 2007, a basking shark was tagged. She swam all the way from the United Kingdom to Canada. So it seems basking sharks don't hibernate after all – they migrate!

Some great white sharks are known to swim 1,500 miles from California to the middle of the Pacific Ocean, but no one knows why. They might be hunting mysterious giant squid that live deep in the Pacific. Records say no human has ever seen a giant squid alive!

So how do sharks find their way around in the water? Well, they use their senses...

Five facts about shark senses

• HEARING – sharks have ears inside their bodies and are listening for changes in the water around them all the time. They can hear a wounded animal struggling in the water.

• **TASTE — sharks don't have tongues, but they do have taste buds in their mouths. The mandarin shark trails its feelers, or barbels, along the ocean floor as it swims. It's looking for anything that tastes like food.**

• TOUCH – sharks don't have hands, so they feel things with their mouths and throats. And though their skin is tough, they can feel something touching it.

• **SMELL — a large shark can sniff out a seal best if it's wounded! It's thought a great white shark can smell a drop of blood three miles away!**

• SIGHT – sharks have eyes on the sides of their heads. They can see in water as well as we can see on land. Their eyes are truly amazing...

Facts about sharp-sighted sharks

5. The deeper a shark lives in the ocean, the bigger its eyes. The bigeye thresher shark has eyes bigger than tennis balls!

4. The eyes of a great white shark are a beautiful turquoise blue.

3. Some sharks have an extra eyelid! It's called a 'nictating membrane' and it covers the eye for protection. Sharks attack live animals, which often fight back. The membrane protects the eye from the teeth and claws of a struggling animal. Sharks that don't have the extra eyelid roll back their eyes when they bite.

2. Shark eyes are super-sensitive. In bright light dark

cells cover the back of the eye to protect it from harmful rays - like built-in reactolite glasses!

1. The Greenland shark is often blind because of a tiny creature that lives on its eyes. But, like all sharks, it can still feel its way around in the water...

DO YOU KNOW?

Sharks have an extra sense that we don't have. Get close to a shark and you might notice lots of small dots around its head. They are called: ampullae of Lorenzini. These dots are really holes filled with a sort of jelly. They help sharks to pick up electrical pulses that come from an animal's heartbeat. They make it easier for sharks to search out hidden creatures in the dark.

It's touching!

The lateral line runs from a shark's mouth all the way down to the tip of its tail. It works a bit like our sense of touch, so sharks can feel changes in the water around them. The lateral line helps a shark to...

- **keep away from its enemies**
- **get close to its dinner**
- **avoid bumping into things.**

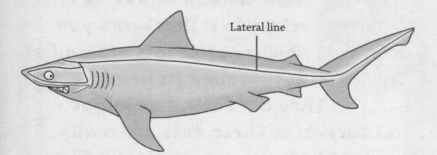

Lateral line

Senses also help sharks migrate thousands of miles. Some sharks migrate to have babies. Some lay eggs on the seabed. Most give birth to live pups...

Facts about shark babies

5. The horn shark lays corkscrew-shaped eggs. It takes up to two hours to lay each one, but the egg wedges neatly between rocks, so it stays in one place, away from harm.

4. A swellshark lays eggs with strings, or tendrils, at the corners. The tendrils tangle in seaweed so the egg won't drift away.

3. Mako shark eggs hatch inside the mum. The babies fatten up on extra eggs she makes for them before they are born.

2. Babies in the womb of a sand tiger shark eat extra eggs, and each other! It's the only food they have, so only the biggest, strongest pups survive.

1. Whale sharks have the most babies. One mum was found with 300 pups in her womb!

Sharks are often born tail first. The hammerhead shark first pops into the water with the sides of its head folded back. All sharks start hunting straight away. They have to look after themselves, because shark mums make terrible parents. If a baby doesn't swim away fast, its mum might eat it!

Sharp facts about shark teeth

3. Shark teeth grow in rows. Some have just five rows, others have 15!

2. The teeth don't have roots, so they can drop out easily. A tooth can drop out after a few weeks or months, but there is always a new one ready to take its place.

Shark's teeth are designed for the food they eat:

• Great white sharks have up to 300 teeth. They are shaped like triangles, with jagged edges. When the top and bottom teeth bite together, there's no gap at all – seal bones and flesh are chomped up quickly!

• Spiny dogfish have flat teeth that grind together. They're good for eating crabs and shellfish. But their edges are sharp and can give fishermen a nasty bite!

• Basking sharks have up to 1,500 teeth! But they are really small. Basking sharks eat lots of tiny creatures, so they don't need to bite.

1. Some sharks will get through 20,000 teeth in a lifetime!

Tongue stones

When a shark dies, its cartilage skeleton rots quickly, so shark fossils are hard to find. However, fossils of shark's teeth *have* been found in rocks.

People thought that the teeth looked like little tongues and that they formed naturally in the rock. For years, they believed these 'tongue stones' had special powers!

Women kept them by their beds for luck when they gave birth

People hung them on the backs of doors to keep snakes and scorpions away

People dipped them in wine as a protection against poisoning!

In 1666, a Danish scientist, called Nicholas Steno, realized the stones were really shark's teeth. He was looking at the cut-off head of a very large shark at the time. He also worked out that the tongue stones actually came from extinct sharks, and that the land where they were found had once been covered by sea.

Great white shark facts

So which is the biggest fish in the ocean? It isn't the great white shark ... but the great white *is* the biggest meat-eating fish!

5. When it's born, a great white shark is about as big as a ten-year-old boy.

4. A full-grown shark can be 6.4 metres long. It's around 2.4 metres wide and 1.8 metres deep!

3. It's only the great white's tummy that is white. Looking up from under the water, a great white shark is very hard to see. It has a grey top-coat for camouflage from above.

2. Baby whites eat fish, but dinner gets bigger as the shark grows longer. From seals, to sea lions, to dolphins, to elephant seals and even whales — though the whales are usually dead already!

1. Great whites don't need to eat all the time. A shark that has feasted on a dead whale might not feed again for a month!

THE TOP 4

Important things to know about basking sharks

4. A basking shark can grow to be nearly twice the size of a great white shark and weighs just under 5,000 kilograms!

3. Even though they're big, basking sharks don't hunt huge prey. Instead, they eat plankton: tiny plants, animals and eggs that float in the water.

2. Most sharks have mouths underneath their bodies, but a basking shark's mouth is at the front. It's nearly a metre wide!

1. The basking shark swims with its huge mouth open most of the time. This is because it's feeding. As it swims forward, it forces water into its mouth, where gillrakers filter out the food. The water then passes out of the body through the gills.

This is hard work...

But the basking shark isn't the biggest fish in the ocean...

Whale shark facts

5. The whale shark really is the biggest fish in the sea – the longest ever measured was over 12 metres long. That's about as long as a basking shark, but a whale shark is wider and much, much heavier. It weighs between nine and 20 tonnes!

4. A whale shark mouth is up to 1.5 metres wide. It could probably swallow you sideways! But this shark wouldn't want to eat you.

3. Like basking sharks, whale sharks are filter feeders. But they don't need to swim forward to eat. Instead they suck in small fish and plankton, a bit like a vacuum cleaner!

2. You can tell one whale shark from another by the pattern

of light spots on its dark skin.
Scientists can use the same
computer programme they use to
search out stars in the sky to map
the skin patterns of a whale shark.

1. Experts think some whale sharks might
live for up to 150 years.

Mmm, yummy, plankton

But there was once a much bigger fish...

Meet Megalodon

Actually, no human ever did meet megalodon, but that's probably for the best! Megalodon swam in most of the world's oceans 15 million years ago. It died out around two million years ago. It's probably the biggest shark, or fish, that EVER lived.

We only know about megalodon because of its fossilized teeth. No other remains have ever been found. The teeth are like great white shark teeth, but much, much bigger! The name Megalodon means 'big tooth'.

A great white shark's tooth is around 6 centimetres long. But megalodon teeth have been found measuring up to 21 centimetres! Experts think megalodon was 18 metres long and weighed around 45 tonnes! Its mouth was probably 2 metres wide. It could have eaten a great white shark for breakfast!

Megalodon tooth **Great white shark tooth**

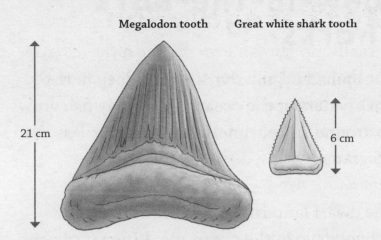

21 cm

6 cm

We do know that megalodon ate whale meat. How? Because whale fossils have been found that are millions of years old – and they have megalodon-sized bite marks on them!

Not all sharks are enormous. Some are surprisingly small...

Glow-in-the-dark sharks

The spined pygmy shark swims deep in the dark waters of the ocean. This titchy fish grows to around 23 centimetres and weighs less than 25 grams.

The dwarf lanternshark is even smaller! It lives deep in the ocean too. When it's born it measures just 6 centimetres and grows to around 18 centimetres.

These sharks may be small, but they share one very special feature – a glow-in-the-dark tum!

Tiny fish swim towards the mini sharks' tummies. They think they're coming up to the surface of the water.

Bigger fish look for dark shapes to attack in the water. The light-up tummies confuse them ... and they swim away!

Oooooooh!

At around a metre long, the swellshark is a small shark. It has a special feature though. When an enemy is circling, the swellshark wedges itself in a crack in the rocks. Then it swallows loads of water and swells up to look twice as big as normal!

Surprising shark habits

Sharks of all shapes and sizes behave in unusual ways...

6. Epaulette sharks can walk! They use their muscly fins to stroll along the seabed as they search for crabs and snails.

5. The dark shyshark grows to just 24 centimetres. When danger threatens, it curls its tail right over its eyes for protection!

4. Wobbegong sharks are also called carpet sharks, because they have fancy, patterned skin with frills around the edges. Wobbegongs lie still on the bottom of the ocean so that they are very hard to see. They don't move as their dinner floats past, they just suck it in!

3. When basking sharks swim round in a circle, nose to tail, it's called 'cartwheeling'! Some people believe it's to do with mating, but groups of female sharks do it without a male in sight.

2. Great white sharks sometimes swim upright, pop their great jaws out of the water and have a good look around. It's called spy-hopping, but most surprising of all...

1. ...is that sharks sometimes fly! Enormous great white sharks can leap right out of the water, or 'breach'. When a great white zooms in on a seal it moves very, very fast. Sometimes it catches the seal, keeps on going forward, breaks through the water and flies through the air!

Sharks never sleep. They have to keep moving their gills to let oxygen flow through their body. Some sharks have to keep swimming even when they're resting. Others can rest on the ocean floor, but they don't sleep like humans do. Instead of 'switching off', sharks just slow down. Even when they're resting on a rock, or on the seabed, a shark's eyes never close. They will still follow an object moving in the water.

Deadly sharks

Not all sharks will attack you. Some are more dangerous than others. But watch out for...

3. Bull sharks – at two metres long these sharks aren't so big, but bull sharks are bullies. They often headbutt an animal before eating it. One bull shark victim said the headbutt was like being hit by a lorry! Bull sharks can swim in waters that aren't very deep, so they get closer to people than most other sharks.

SHALLOW WATER

2. Tiger sharks — can grow to nearly five metres long. These sharks get their name from the stripes on their skin. They swim lazily along in the water, but when they spot something to eat, they zoom in at 20 miles an hour. Tiger sharks' teeth are razor sharp for crunching sea turtle shells. Because they can crunch through anything, tiger sharks will eat anything, so it's best to keep out of their way.

There's no prize for guessing that the deadliest sharks are...

1. Great white sharks – When a great white strikes, it pulls back its head and pushes its jaws forward. Its bottom teeth hit first. Then the upper teeth slice downwards. It has to move its whole head from side to side to cut off a piece of flesh.

Like other sharks, the great white's jaws are attached to its skull by muscles, not by bone. A great white bite is powerful, but because the jaws aren't part of the skeleton, its body doesn't feel the force of the bite.

Great whites can be fussy about food. They usually take a test bite first, then swim away. If you're an otter, a sea bird, or a human, you're far too bony. The shark will usually leave you alone. If you're a nice blubbery seal, the great white can get lots of energy from your fat. It will watch while you slowly bleed to death, then zoom in for supper.

Great white sharks have
tail-splashing contests!
Two sharks slap their
tails hard on the surface
of the water. The shark
that makes the biggest
splash wins.

Do You Know?

Will it eat me?
Facts and figures

• There are 300 to 400 types of shark in the world's oceans.

• Around 50 types of shark have attacked humans at some time.

•Twelve types of shark have killed people.

• Shark attacks have been recorded for over 400 years.

• There have been nearly 1,400 shark attacks on humans in that time.

• Around 140 people died because of those attacks.

• Every year, 70-100 attacks are recorded in the whole world. Only 5-15 people die.

• Every year, more people are struck by lightning than are killed by sharks. And, of course, the sea has other dangers.

• In the United States in 2000, 74 people drowned at the seaside — only one person was killed by a shark that year.

• The hotspots for shark attacks are Florida in the United States, South Africa and Australia, but even in those waters your risk of attack is very low.

THE TOP 6

Shark safety tips

It's a good idea to keep your distance from any shark. So use these tips to make sure you're safe in the water...

6. Don't go swimming in the early morning or early evening, when the light is dim. This is when sharks like to hunt.

5. Don't wear stripy clothes, or bright jewellery. A shark might mistake you for a fish! Keep your swimming gear dark and plain.

4. Don't splash about in deep water – a shark might think you're a wounded seal.

3. Don't go near other animals in the water — sharks may be chasing them.

2. Don't go in the water if you're bleeding, and don't wee in the water. Remember the shark's sense of smell!

1. Don't swim on your own and never EVER touch, try to feed a shark, or get in its way!

Sharks on the attack

But what if you do find a shark by chance?
How can you tell what it's thinking? Well,
you can try to read a shark's body language.

A spotter's guide

This shark isn't interested in you.

This shark thinks you're its next dinner.

A shark swimming round you in circles, or zig-zagging towards you with fins pointing down is a very bad sign. Most sharks hunch their backs when they are angry. At this point, you don't have much time to get away. Some hunch for 40 seconds. The great white does it for just 3-4 seconds!

Different sharks give different attack signals:

- **a great white shark might swim straight for you, swerving away at the last minute.**
- **a sand tiger shark might beat its tail in the water, making loud cracking noises.**
- **great whites, bull sharks and tiger sharks will swim with their jaws open.**

So what can you do if it does attack?

Ways to handle a shark attack

6. If you spot a shark, get out of the water fast, but try not to panic! Swim smoothly away and the shark might leave you alone.

5. If you're underwater, swim back to back with a friend, then get out fast.

4. If you can't get out, back up against something hard – like a large rock – so the shark can't get at you.

3. Keep watching the shark to see what it's doing.

2. If it comes close, try to find something hard and hit it on the nose. You can hit with your hand, but you don't want to lose your fingers!

1. If the shark gets you in its mouth, fight back with all your might! Go for the eyes, go for the gills on the side of its head, hit where the shark is really going to feel it.

SHARK-
INFESTED
WATERS

The good news is that most people do escape shark attacks...

Survival stories

3. The first account of someone surviving a shark attack was in 1749. Brook Watson was near Havana, Cuba, when he jumped off his ship for a swim. A shark attacked and bit off his lower leg! Brook had to have a wooden leg to replace it, but this didn't hold him back – he later became Lord Mayor of London!

2. Bethany Hamilton started surfing in Hawaii when she was just seven. She was soon winning surfing competitions. Then, in 2003, aged 13, lying on her surfboard, she had her arm bitten off by a tiger shark! She swam calmly to the shore for help. She was surfing again just a few weeks later!

1. In 1963, a man named Rodney Fox was attacked by a great white shark. He escaped death by wrapping himself round the shark's body, so it couldn't bite him. But he was still badly injured. It took 360 stitches to put him back together again. He still has a piece of shark tooth stuck in his wrist!

THE TOP 3

Strangest things found in a shark's tum

3. A porbeagle shark was found with a whole pigeon in its stomach. The pigeon had a ring round its leg, so the fish seller who found the bird phoned its owner to break the news!

2. Tiger sharks eat anything that comes their way. They have been found with bags of coal, car tyres — one was even found with an African drum inside it!

1. Great whites take the biscuit again. Many strange things have been found inside these sharks, including: a cuckoo clock, a reindeer, half a horse, and a man dressed in a full suit of armour!

Do You Know?

Normally when a shark eats something it can't digest, it turns its stomach inside out and pushes the item out of its mouth again. Sharks can also be sick, like we can. They sometimes throw up to chase off an enemy!

You might think it's safest to stay out of the water, but even on dry land, sharks can move in mysterious ways...

Warning — fish out of water!

Three people who got a sharky shock:

• A pub landlady in Kent, England, was injured when a stuffed shark fell off the wall and landed on her!

• Even dead sharks can bite. One driver crashed his car with a dead shark in the back. He flew backwards and landed on the shark's teeth. He needed quite a few stitches!

• British sailor, Paul Stephens, got a shock in a Sydney Aquarium. The shark tank burst, and glass, water, fish and sharks flew everywhere! Paul wasn't bitten by the sharks, but he was badly cut by the flying glass.

Sharks usually attack humans by mistake. They sometimes swallow things by accident too...

Most mysterious sharks

Sharks have some unusual habits, but some sharks are more unusual than others...

The megamouth shark – strangely, this shark was first discovered just over 35 years ago. Since then only 40 have been found. That's probably because it lives deep in the ocean. It grows up to 5.5 metres long.

It's called megamouth because of its wide mouth and its very peculiar lips, which glow in the dark to attract food!

The goblin shark – we don't know much about this four-metre long fish. It's found dead more often than it's found alive. It's thought that the weird horn that juts straight out of its forehead may be lined with sensors. The sensors help this fish to feel its way around in the dark waters of the deep. A goblin shark's skin looks pink, because it is almost see-through!

Goblin sharks are called 'living fossils'. Most creatures evolve, or adapt their bodies, over a long period of time. Scientists think goblin sharks haven't changed in 100 million years!

There are plenty more strange sharks in the sea...

Weirdest-looking sharks

Two of the strangest sharks are the longnose sawshark and the hammerhead shark.

The longnose sawshark's body grows up to 1.4 metres long. And at least a quarter of that is its saw-shaped nose! The nose has about twenty teeth on each side.

A baby sawshark's teeth only flick out after it is born, so the mum is protected during birth.

The sawshark can use its amazing nose to slash at its prey, or to dig up tasty creatures from the seabed.

The hammerhead shark's weird head shape means it can swim better and has more ampullae of Lorenzini (see p. 17). The biggest type of hammerhead shark can grow up to 6 metres long.

Having eyes and nostrils on the sides of its head helps these sharks to see and smell really well. Tests have shown that a hammerhead can see all around it. In fact, the wider apart the eyes, the better! Hammerheads certainly need good eyesight to chase after the speeding stingrays it eats.

Fast fish

It's not easy to measure a shark's speed, but most fishermen agree on which is the fastest:

3. The great white can swim at 25-35 miles per hour (or mph), but only reaches top speed when it zooms in for the kill.

2. A two-metre-long blue shark was recorded swimming at a steady 24.5 mph. In short bursts, it could even reach 43 mph!

1. As mako sharks eat blue sharks, it's safe to say they can swim faster. Growing to around 3 metres long, they can leap out of the water too – up to 6 metres in the air!

It's thought a mako can swim at a steady 30 mph, with bursts of up to 46 mph. Though one researcher claimed a mako reached 68 mph!

Blue sharks and mako sharks can be harmful to humans, but blue sharks are especially dangerous...

It's thought that blue sharks and oceanic whitetips were to blame for...

The bloodiest shark attack EVER...

It happened in 1945, when an American ship — the USS *Indianapolis* — was hit by a Japanese torpedo.

Nine hundred men were thrown into the water. It took four days for rescue to arrive. In that time, 579 men died — many of them eaten by sharks.

Making sure sharks stay away

Scientists have been working on shark repellents ever since the attack on the *Indianapolis*. They've found out that...

• sharks don't like the smell of dead shark. But the smell was difficult to put in a bottle.
• sharks don't like soap. But soap can pollute the sea water.
• electric repellents are too dangerous.

Eau de
dead shark

In 2004, American scientist, Eric Stroud, experimented with a chemical that sends messages between sharks to warn them of danger.

He dropped raw meat into sea water and waited for the sharks to come. Once some sharks were busy feeding, he dropped in the chemical. The sharks swam away in panic!

Repellent could be used on swimsuits and wet suits, but that's not all...

Each year, many sharks are killed or injured in huge nets intended to catch shoals of smaller fish. If the nets were treated with repellent, the sharks might stay well away.

Diving with sharks

Would you really want to get closer to sharks? Well, diving with sharks does attract plenty of tourists!

Instead of looking at sharks through glass, you climb into a cage that's lowered into the water. You can then see dangerous sharks close up, without fear of being attacked.

Cage diving now happens safely around the world, but there have been one or two accidents. One great white shark got trapped in the bars of a cage, and wrecked the cage wall. Luckily, the divers escaped unharmed.

If you really want to dive without the bars, you could try a protective suit. It's made from strong metal mesh, a bit like chainmail that knights used to wear!

Free-diving with sharks

Shark photographer Ron Taylor designed the chainmail suit to wear underwater. But it didn't fit, so he got his wife to wear it instead! To test it out, Valerie Taylor sat on the seabed waiting for the sharks to bite. They didn't! She had to put tuna under the suit to get them to notice her. Meanwhile, husband Ron filmed her. The sharks did bite, and Valerie wasn't harmed.

Luckily, Ron and Valerie Taylor knew what they were doing. They've been free-diving with sharks for over 40 years. Ron has filmed Valerie riding a whale shark, and even feeding a great white – by hand!

Shark man!

Like the Taylors, Mike Rutzen started out fishing for sharks and now campaigns to help save them. By watching them carefully, he has started to understand shark body language and he copies the way they move, so he can swim safely alongside them. Sometimes he hitches a ride! Mike can even hypnotize a shark...

How to hypnotize a shark

1. First find your shark. It's best to start small and work up to bigger sharks. Lemon sharks are ideal, but this works with great whites too!

2. Gently turn your shark on its back, and maybe tickle its nose. Your shark will look like it's sleeping.

3. You now have up to 15 minutes to have a good look at it. Some sharks can be hypnotized for several hours. Scientists can study and even operate on sharks in this state. It's called 'tonic immobility'.

4. Turn it around again, and your shark should swim away.

Mike Rutzen had been studying sharks and swimming with them for a very long time before he tried hypnotizing one!

THE TOP 4

Fishy Friends

4. Remoras are fish that can grow to nearly 1 metre long. They hitch a ride on larger sharks by attaching themselves with suckers on their fins.

3. For pilot fish, swimming with a large shark saves energy. The metre-long fish can also catch scraps of food that fall from the shark's mouth when it's feeding.

2. Tiny cleaner wrasse feed on things like lice, dead skin and barnacles that they find on their shark mates. So the wrasse gets a meal and the shark gets a clean!

1. But sharks are probably best friends with each other. Experts have found that sharks that swim together in groups have larger brains than sharks that live on their own. They think lemon sharks may be able to recognize and learn things from each other.

◎ Best buddies ◎

Scientists can recognize a shark by fin-printing! The dorsal fin (see p. 5) of each shark is different in shape, size and pattern from any other dorsal fin in the ocean.

Creatures that can scare a shark

Considering how dangerous they are, sharks don't have as many enemies as you might think...

5. Dolphins will fight a shark, if they feel threatened. They ram into its gills for self-defence.

4. If a shark tries to eat a 60-cm-long puffer fish it gets a nasty surprise. When it senses danger, this fish swallows water and puffs itself up into a large, spiky ball. On top of that, it's deadly to all sharks except the tiger shark!

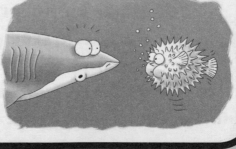

3. Sharks eat each other! Larger sharks eat smaller sharks, and some sharks even feed on their own kind.

2. Then there is the killer whale, or orca. By slapping its tail on the water, the orca whips up a whirlpool that brings a shark to the water's surface. It turns the shark onto its back, with a flip of its tail. The shark is hypnotized and the orca can eat it without a fight.

But there is one creature that is much more dangerous to sharks...

1. Man! Each year, 75 million sharks are killed – one every three seconds! Some are killed for food – rock salmon is a type of shark used for fish and chips. Others are killed to make medicines that may even not work. But most are killed just for their fins...

Shark's fin soup has been a special Chinese dish for hundreds of years. People serve it to show respect to guests and to show that they have money. The soup can be delicious, but the shark's fin itself is flavourless. Because it is so popular, shark fins are worth lots of money. Shark meat is not. Fishermen will catch any shark, large or small, rare or common. They cut off the fins and throw the body back into the sea. Sometimes the shark is still alive!

Countries are slowly changing their laws to make shark 'finning' illegal. But to make a difference, they need to act fast.

Sharks in Danger

For every 100 great white sharks that used to swim in our seas, there are now just 20 left.

For every 100 hammerhead sharks there are just 11 left.

In one part of Cornwall, fishermen once caught 6,000 sharks per year. They now catch fewer than 200.

Sharks have been around for 400 million years. They swam in our seas before the dinosaurs came and before the first tree grew. Now they are in danger, and humans are to blame. By the end of this century, there could be no sharks in our seas at all!

Should we worry more about sharks attacking us, or our attacks on sharks?

What do you think?

Sharks Quiz

1. **The biggest shark EVER, was:**
a) the great white
b) the whale shark
c) megalodon.

2. **If a shark attacks you, you should:**
a) stay put and splash about in the water
b) swim away swiftly, keeping the shark in sight at all times
c) turn it onto its back and give it a kiss.

3. **Tongue stones are:**
a) fossilized shark's teeth.
b) bits of bone that get stuck in a shark's tongue
c) ancient statues made by shark worshippers.

4. The scales on a shark's skin are called:

    a) gills

    b) denticles

    c) fins

5. Bull sharks have been found:

    a) on top of a wardrobe

    b) in the deepest part of the ocean

    c) up the Ganges river, in India.

6. Barbels are:

    a) a type of shark moustache

    b) feelers that help a shark find food

    c) a shark's favourite food.

7. Before they are born baby tiger sharks:

    a) are taken to special shark nurseries

    b) eat their mother's womb

    c) eat each other.

DANGER SHARKS

8. Epaulette sharks use their fins to:

a) walk along the seabed
b) feed themselves
c) scratch their backs.

9. A great white's favourite food is:

a) a nice juicy child
b) an nice tasty otter
c) a nice blubbery seal.

10. The first recorded shark victim survived and:

a) took up shark taming
b) became Lord Mayor of London
c) ate the shark that bit him.